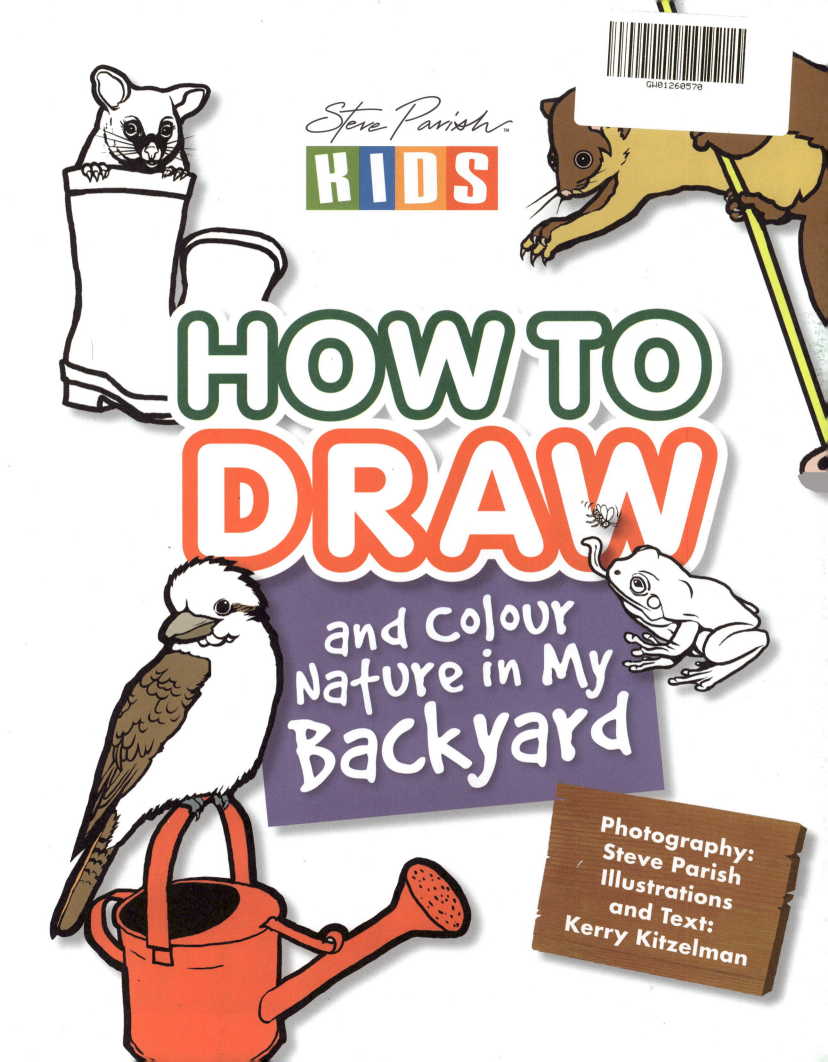

DRAWING & COLOURING
IN MY BACKYARD

Children learn how to draw over a long period, starting from their very first scribbles (usually on a wall somewhere), and for some, drawing will develop into a life-long occupation. At the very least, those early pre-school scratchings will help to develop the necessary hand–eye coordination required for writing in the later years. This book aims to introduce a little structure to your child's scratchings and perhaps fine tune some of the coordination between their eyes, brain and pencil. Each section begins with a colouring activity and is followed by a simple drawing or tracing exercise.

All colouring pages have a completed "counterpart opposite" so the child can see what colours can be used. Providing a coloured page allows your child to identify colours, match one of their colouring utensils to the colour required then apply it to the page. This process not only helps them recognise and name colours but also requires them to make a decision with respect to their choice of colouring pencil or paint. Often their pencil's colour is not a perfect match, so they choose the closest. In so doing they recognise that shades and tones can exist within the one colour family. The intent of providing a coloured page is certainly not to limit their creativity, but to allow them to make decisions and thus develop decision-making skills.

The tracing activities require your child to draw a controlled series of lines with curves, arches, loops and points (as opposed to the back-and-forth motion of a colouring pencil). Both skills are important. The tracing activities help to develop the coordination necessary for the pencil tip to stay within a narrow path and promotes both medium and fine motor skills.

1. Hold the pencil between your thumb, index and middle fingers.
2. Hold your other fingers under your palm and rest your hand comfortably on the table or writing surface.
3. Hold the pencil about 1–2 cm from the tip.
4. Rest your forearm lightly on the table. Do not bear too much of your upper body weight.

PENCIL GRIP

A backyard fence is no problem for a wombat. It digs a tunnel underneath!

Go away
WOMBAT
sleeping

Kookaburra loves to sit and watch while it waits for breakfast.

Draw kookaburra sitting on the branch by tracing over the grey lines. Then look at the photo to help colour your drawing.

Possum likes to sleep in a hole in a tree, or some other hiding place around the house!

Draw the possum by tracing over the grey lines. Then colour your drawing like the photograph.

Brightly coloured rainbow lorikeet drinks nectar from flowers in the backyard.

Ringtail possum nests in the roof. It is very good at climbing and balancing.

Frog catches insects around the house. You can sometimes hear it croaking in the drain pipes.

Bandicoot is hard to see because it comes out at night. Sometimes it leaves holes in the lawn after digging for worms.

Draw the koalas on page 1 into the picture above. There are no grey lines to help you this time.